PARTICIPATORY RURAL APPRAISAL
IN
AGRICULTURE AND ANIMAL HUSBANDRY

A Training Manual

By the Same Authors

Technology Integration Through Agro-Eco System Analysis : Using Participatory Approaches

---

About the Authors

Dr. (Miss) Shagufta Jamal is a Reader in Department of Adult and Continuing Education and Extension, Jamia Millia Islamia Central University, New Delhi. Earlier she worked as Research Associate in a Ford Foundation-funded Project; Teaching Associate at G.B. Pant University of Agriculture and Technology, Pantnagar; and in Division of Extension Education and at Krishi Vigyan Kendra (KVK), Indian Veterinary Research Institute, Izatnagar.

Dr. Jamal has been the recipient of University Merit Certificate Award during 1975-76. She has been honoured with the Young Scientist Award in 1998 and National Award named ISEE Fellow Award in 2003 by Indian Society of Extension Education for her outstanding work in extension research and field extension activities.

Dr. Jamal has to her credit a book, *Women in Dairy Development* and over three dozen papers. She has also presented two dozen of papers in national and international seminars and conferences.

Dr. H.P.S. Arya is the Head of Division and Joint Director (Extension Education) at Indian Veterinary Research Institute, Izatnagar, Bareilly (U.P.). Starting his professional career in 1963 as Professor & Head, Department of Agricultural Extension at one of the Agricultural College in UP, he has worked in various organizations and in various capacities during his career of 40 years.

Dr. Arya has worked on various country-wide projects, such as Communication in Development Administration, Functioning of Village Level Workers, Study on Satellite-T.V. Experiment while working at NIRD, Hyderabad. While working at IVRI, he has worked in the World Bank funded projects including NATP-Project on Collection, Documentation and Validation of Indigenous Technical Knowledge (ITK) as Zonal Leader. He has visited Australia and Japan in connection with training courses and study mission.

Dr. Arya has published six books, more than 60 research papers, more than 100 technical bulletins and leaflets. He has presented more than 50 research papers in national and international seminars and conferences. He has been the recipient of ISEE Fellow Award of Indian Society of Extension Education.

PARTICIPATORY RURAL APPRAISAL IN AGRICULTURE AND ANIMAL HUSBANDRY

A Training Manual

Shagufta Jamal
H.P.S. Arya

CONCEPT PUBLISHING COMPANY, NEW DELHI-110059

ISBN: 81-8069-117-9 (P.B.)

First Published 2004

Published and Printed by
Ashok Kumar Mittal
Concept Publishing Company
A/15-16, Commercial Block, Mohan Garden
NEW DELHI - 110059 (India)

Phones : 25351460, 25351794
Fax : 091-11-25357103
Email : publishing@conceptpub.com

Preface

Huge amount of technologies have been developed by the Agricultural Research System during the last few decades. Application of technologies have led to achieve green revolution, yellow revolution, white revolution and blue revolution. Inspite of rapid growth in production, the benefits could not be harnessed by all the farmers and at all places. Further, the sustainability of growth has been as another problem. There was a belief that technologies are scale neutral. Of late it has been realized that it is inappropriate technologies which is the key factor responsible for uneven adoption and non-adoption with resource poor farmers having complex, diverse and risk prone farming situations. The technologies are not matching with these situations. This warrants proper identification and selection of technologies matching to the farming situations, testing them at the local level and refine them to suit the situations. This requires proper understanding of the production systems both at macro and micro-levels.

Understanding the farming situations in an specific area is not an easy task. The conventional survey techniques are highly costly, at times unreliable and becomes outdated in the informations at the time of use. With the result any plan based on survey data becomes unrealistic and misleading.

Participatory Rural Appraisal (PRA) method has been evolved through a number of experiments which has now been considered most appropriate to understand and analyse the local situations in the shortest time frame with adequate reliability. The method was an improvement over the Rapid

Rural Appraisal (RRA) in the sense that it seeks active participation of farmers not only at the later stage but also in taking initiative by the farmers.

Participatory Rural Appraisal technique is not only the knowledge but involves skill and art with conscious effort for seeking farmers' initiative. The survey rely most on the farmers' responses while RRA and PRA rely more on the researcher in collecting and analysing the information by seeking full initiative by the farmers. Training of researchers is necessary for correct application of this technique. Since PRA itself seeks variations in methodologies there have been numerous modifications and with the results dozens of tools have been developed.

It has been observed that simple training of one week or fortnight is not sufficient for a researcher to be effective at work. He requires constant guidance at its use in the field. In the absence of such expert guidance in the field which is not possible in the field technique has the risk of incorrect use, leading to misleading information. So far no handy and simple literature is available which could be used in the field as practical guide while using PRA method.

The present manual on PRA will fill up this gap and will serve as guide and tool in the hands of the researcher in the use of this new method of collecting and analysing information on farming systems. A trained researcher may use this manual as readily available reference to check and verify the PRA tool for its correct use. The standardised tools of PRA could be used in the original form to avoid the dilution of seriousness on the part of investigator.

The Manual has three parts. The first part provides basic and practical understanding of PRA method. This includes features of PRA, its principles, steps, guidelines and types. The second part provides steps and practical guidelines for using major PRA tools under four categories, viz. space analysis, time analysis, seasonal analysis and matrix analysis. In addition, few other PRA tools have been given. While listing the steps and practical guidelines, supportive illustrations and examples have been given which could provide a check to the investigator in the field itself. The third part provides steps of participatory planning on the basis of collected information in respect of identification and prioritization of problems, problem cause analysis, identification of intervention points and their possible alternative solutions.

The present Manual will be useful for the researchers, investigators and field workers involved in rural development, students of rural and allied developments, planners in making realistic plans and administrators for quick understanding of the rural situations.

This Manual has been possible and has been the result of the active participation of the villagers of Dohna, Kamua, Manda and Purenatal in Bareilly district (U.P.) with their full initiative. The authors greatly acknowledge their contributions. The author's have no words of appreciation of the painstaking efforts of the publisher M/s Concept Publishing Co., New Delhi especially the personal and emotional encouragements given by Shri Ashok Mittal, which have made this desire fulfilled.

Shagufta Jamal
H.P.S. Arya

Contents

Introduction

Agricultural Research system has generated vast knowledge for synthesis of appropriate technologies for the farmers and liverstock owners. There was a belief that technologies synthesised in the field of agriculture and animal science are resource and scale neutral. The majority of Indian farmers have very small holdings having less than two hectares of land. Similarly majority of livestock owners have very small units with one or two cows or buffaloes for milk production; one or two goat for goat milk and meat and two to five poultry birds for eggs and one or two pigs for pig production.

Of late, it has been realised that it is inappropriate technologies which is very key factor in non-adoption specially with resource poor and small production units. The technologies generated at research system are not appropriate, suitable and applicatble to the socio-economic and cultural situations of the small production system which are highly complex, diverse and risk-prone. The technologies are not matching with their farming situations.

Technology testing and development for small, diverse, complex and risk- prone production systems must begin with agro eco-system analysis through which the micro and macro level situations centred around agriculture and animals must be listed and apprised of. These may include the land use pattern, cropping systems, varieties and inputs used, pests and diseases and productivity in agriculture as well as species, the breed, the production potentiality, the land & water, housing and other physical resoures, the feeding system, breeding strategies and patterns, the health status, disease pattern, input and labour availability, production processing and marketing etc in livestock production system.

Participatory Rural Appraisal (PRA) method has been considered the most appropriate to understnad and analyse the local situations.

Proper understanding of the farmers and livestock owners, their situations, problems and solutions from their point of view has always been the challenge before the scientists, social scientists, extension workers, development workers, specially in democratic countries like ours. The conventional survey method provided detail and comprehensive information on desired aspects. But, the approach was quite time consuming so much so that by the time the results of survey are available in usable manner, they become obsolete, out dated and false in rapid changing society. Moreover, the man being an intelligent manipulator towards own interest and perception, the reliability of the data was many times questionable.

Dissatisfaction with the results of long-term baseline survey as well as unstructured and superficial short term studies, prompted a search for more cost effective and above all more realistic methods during the last decade. The Rapid Rural Appraisal (RRA) methods began to emerge in the last 1970s which can be defined as a systematic; semi-structured activity conducted on site by multidisciplinary team with the aim of quickly and efficiently acquiring new information and hypothesis about usual life and natural resources. For agriculture and animal science problem the team should consist of one animal scientist, one agronomist, one extension education expert and one economist. It would be better if one lady scientist is included in the team to ensure participation of rural women.

In the mid-1980s the words, participation and participatory entered the RRA vocabulary. The new approach was termed as Participatory Rural Appraisal (PRA) started in India and spread to countries all over the world. PRA is a way of enabling local people to analyze their living conditions and to share the outcomes. The methodology has been developed as an alternative and to complement conventional sample survey methodology and hence should not be considered as a substitute for the survey research.

List of Figures

1

Understanding PRA

PRA is a way of learning from and with villagers to investigate, analyse and evaluate constraints and opportunities.It is the methodology for assessing the problem and needs of farmers and livestock owners by involving them in the whole process of problem identification; determining the solution; developing the action plan to solve the problem followed by implementation. PRA is flexible and adaptable need assessment technique modified by a researcher according to the local context. It is fully participatory in nature unlike the other research methods wherein the researchers or team of researchers pay a small visit to the rural areas and identify the needs of farmers and livestock owners based on their own perception.

Features of PRA

1. *Triangulation* : This is a form of cross -checking by changing the team composition, the sources of information and the techniques applied. There is need that each activity or phenomenon is considered from different viewpoints and studied using different techniques.

The diversity in PRA scientist's team and also in villager group having different interest groups help in triangulation and thereby in higher reliability of information.

2. *Learning in the community* : PRA is an approach for learning from, with and through members of the local community. The PRA scientists team should make all possible efforts to see the situation through the eyes of the affected people. To achieve this the team members must become friendly to the villagers by taking part in their every day

activities and by listening and learning from them.

3. *Optimal Ignorance and Appropriate - Imprecision :* In conventional survey, efforts are made to collect information on all possible aspects very exhaustively and most of the time only a part of it is used. On the contrary in PRA approach the information is generated only on the aspects which are directly required in accordance with the aims and objectives of the study. Further, an effort is made to avoid unnecessary precision during the process of collection and analysis of data.

4. *Use of Appropriate tools / techniques* : The selection of tools / techniques needs to be done carefully. Tools should be simlple, clear, self evident and appropriate to local conditions. The team should also be ready for any modification in the technique that might be suggested by the residents of the study area. Appropriate means and local materials may be taken for describing quantities and qualities and setting-up classification schemes.

5. *On Site Analysis* : The team should meet each evening to jointly discuss and analyse that day's findings and also to plan the work to be done on the following day. The repeated on the spot analysis enable them to understand the existing situation, concentrate on the problem areas and lead to growing understanding and accumulation of knowledge. The results should be evaluated by the team before departure from the area and should be publicly presented and discussed with members of the community.

6. *Offsetting Biases, self-critical awareness* : This process should try to have involvement - of those who would otherwise never get a chance to speak, the poorest people, women, disadvantaged groups in remote areas etc. still important is that the team must refrain from any value judgements about others.

7. *Multi-disciplinary Team* : The scientific team conducting

PRA must have fairly broad base, meaning thereby inclusion of scientists of all important disciplines relevant to the area of study. It is also important to have female scientists in the team so that rural women could be effectively involved in the appraisal exercise.

The team should identify among themselves one member who should work as Team Leader/ Facilitator. Another member should be identified to work as Process Recorder or Content Recorder. While interacting with the villagers he/she should not jump directly to the objective of the study but first develop rapport with them. The responsibility of rapport building may be assigned to one member of the team who could work as Environment Controller.

Principles of PRA

- Congenial attitudes and friendly behaviour with villagers.
- Outsider (scientist) as listener and villager as teacher
- Facilitating
- Sharing
- Reversal of learning
- learning rapidly and progressively
- Seeking diversity
- Triangulation
- Self Critical awareness and commitment

Approach of PRA

L Listen to what they say
E Encourage them to join the discussion
A Ask question (do not make judgements)
R Review what has been discussed
N Note what has been discussed.

Steps of PRA

1. *Direct observaton* : Direct observation has no substitute to collect the reliable data from the primary source since it provides proof in itself. The team members, therefore, must always act as observer through out the PRA exercise. Valuable hints and information should be collected by critically observing the objects and acts right from entering into the area. Each observation must be recorded as early as possible. The critical analysis of these obervations/notes will not only provide the additional information but will help in triangulation.

2. *Rapport buildng* : The first most requirement of PRA is rapport building and environment creation for free and frank interaction by the villagers. The best way to achieve this condition is that the team members during the study period stay and eat with local people. The team should listen and take part in every day activities.

3. *DIY (Do-It Yourself)* : The team members should make efforts to perform the activities that the villagers are doing such as sowing the seeds, transplanting, harvesting, threshing, feeding the animals, milking, chaffing the fodder etc. This helps not only in rapport building but provides practical ideas and feelings of complexities of activities.

4. *SSI (Semi-Structured Interview)* : This is the most important and critical step of PRA process. The individuals are asked relevant but informal questions. No structured schedule or questionnaire is prepared for interviewing. Various roles, such as team leader, process recorder and environment controllers are divided among the members of PRA team. The team should be well prepared before entering into the village.

5. *Focus - Group Interviews* : Group interviews are always better than individual interview. It provides exhaustive information with all possible triangulation and does not leave

any chance of missing information. Focus group interviews are arranged under special circumstances depending upon the specific objectives of the study. Focus group interviews provide specific and pointed data for the specific group without any intervention, hindrance and hesitation from other villagers not belonging to the focus group. Separate focus group interviews may be arranged for women, for weaker sections, for paddy growers, for sugarcane growers, for dairy farmers and so on.

Guidelines for Designing PRA

1. Break down the complex process into small steps and parts and develop and deal with each step and part in turn keeping in mind the whole process.
2. Distinguish clearly different levels, topics, sub-topics, questions and indicators to avoid confusion during the field work.
3. Start with something easy to make the informants relaxed.
4. Run through a list of questions while designing a PRA such as what, why, who, for whom, how, where, when, what for, which, with what etc.
5. Review secondary sources, interview key informants and use your own knowledge and logic to identify topics, key issues and to formulate hypothesis.
6. Move from general to the specific and from material to ideological topics. Leave sensisitive issues untill the end.
7. Think of analysis early. Use analytical tools through out PRA.
8. Think of ways of involving community members in the analysis of information.

Guidelines for PRA Fieldwork

1. Use at least four days but not more than three weeks.
2. Use a small team with good mix of background and interests.
3. Choose a team leader.
4. Use the information, which has already been collected earlier.
5. Triangulate the methods, the team and the information sources.
6. Discuss the objectives of the PRA with community leaders at site.
7. Start the field work by asking broad background information.
8. Start with something simple.
9. Identify and carefully select community members and key informants. The size of sample depends on the homogenity and size of the community and the topic. In complex urban areas, a larger sample is needed than in rural areas, but in most cases 20 to 50 informants should be sufficient.
10. Combine interview with direct observation.
11. Use key indicators and checklists during direct observations.
12. Use key indicators as short events.
13. Only ask relevant questions.
14. Adopt yourself and your plan which suit to the community members.
15. Conduct interview individually and in groups.
16. After the first round of interviews and observations and at least in the evening, keep time to meet the team members and discuss finding and review.
17. Do case studies of households to identify variations.
18. Allow time for team interaction.

19. Make a plan for every following day of field work.
20. Rotate the role of team members. Shuffle the members of the interviewing groups if possible.
21. Refine, modify and experiment with different tools.
22. Combine different methods and experiment with different sequences of methods.
23. Keep the team ready to face unpredictable situation and turn constraints into opportunities.
24. Have second and third meetings with the same people.
25. Present your analysis to key informants to confirm and cross check.
26. Look, listen and learn. Don't lecture.
27. Don't hide mistakes but share them and correct them from others.
28. Be self critical. Ask questions yourself.
29. Stay with the community. If not possible, be around in the evenings, at dinner and in the morning.
30. Allow sufficient time for team interaction.
31. Every day, schedule the time for writing field notes.
32. Show interest in learning from the people.
33. Mix with the community members. Respect the community members and their knowledge.
34. Experiment with different forms of community participation.
35. Don't concentrate only on one segment of community. Include women and children.
36. The findings of PRA must be believable.

Types of PRA

PRA can be of different types:

1. Deductive PRA
2. Topical PRA
3. Exploratory PRA

4. Planning & Implementing PRA
5. Monitoring and Evaluative PRA

1. *Deductive PRA*: Deductive PRA is used when the problem that requires tact and can not be directly handled such as ethnic violence, communal riots and corruption etc. These problems can be studied through relating them different aspcts of village life rather than treating them through direct probing. For instance, if one wants to study the causes of communal tension, direct questions will not reveal exact causes. But PRA sessions on different aspects of village life related to communal tensions would give indications of the causes

2. *Topical PRA* :For topical PRA, the sessions have to be on particular topic. For instance, if one has to study the crop or animal diseases, PRA can help in exploring different dimensions of diseases. A topic can be probed across different groups in a village, across gender, caste etc. Its purpose is to generate as much information as possible on a selected topic. It is intensive in its approach and can help in analysis of a particular topic at great length.

3. *Exploratory PRA* : The exploratory PRA are used to reveal different aspects of rural life and also suggest important issues to be probed. It can form a basis for further probing into selected areas which appear important and useful. A theme for further analysis can emerge out of such exploration which can help in undertaking either a PRA exercise or help in framing a survey questionnaire on realistic lines.

4. *Planning and Implementing PRA* : PRA can be done for designing project and implementing them. It can make projects more adaptable to local needs. If village communities are involved in a project right from its beginning, the chance of success of the projects increase through people's

participation. PRA seeks commitment from the people for executing the project as partners.

5. *Monitoring and evaluative PRA* : PRA sessions in the village communities can be done for monitoring and evaluation of projects and development programes. With identification of problems, operation of projects can be better informed and solution to any problem can be sought for. In case of problematic situations, monitoring through PRA can bring different groups in the villages together for solving the problems.

2

Understanding Farmers and Livestock Owners : Use of PRA Tools

Knowledge of rural people constitutes the base for the socio - economic and agro-ecological information. The rural people have their experiences, their history and culture, their ideas, their priorities and preferences. Listening to rural people helps them in portraying their point of view which otherwise remain unknown. The three basic foundations of PRA are (i) attitudes and behaviour, (ii) methods and (iii) sharing. Each of these is incomplete without the other. Since PRA is essentially in a participatory mode, the attitudes and behaviour required are those which are favourable to participation. Without such participation, PRA is not feasible. An outsider will not be able to know and understand the systems within which the rural people operate without participation.

PRA Tools

Four patterns are normally chosen to reveal the key functional relationship that determine the properties of an agro-eco system. These are space analysis, time analysis, seasonal analysis and matrix ranking. These analyses provide an understanding about the properties and the process of human management of agro-eco system.

Space Analysis

The spatial patterns are mostly revealed by maps and transects. The functional relationship can be depicted through various maps (social map, resource map, occupational map etc.), while transects are useful in defining a system boundaries and in identifying problem areas.

Mapping Steps

* Ask the villagers to draw the map of their own village at a suitable place which is convenient for all the villagers (dry, visible and spacious place if so that - many people can look at it easily)
* Allow them to draw the map in their own way and don't suggest.
* Don't interrupt from outside.
* There could be 5-6 or more numbers of villagers preparing the map of the village at a time. More the participation of villagers better the quality of map.
* Triangulate the information indicated in the map. Ask some of the villagers to point out his/her house, crop field, orchards, etc. on the map.
* Ask others if they would like to add anything in the map.
* Transfer the map on a paper. A legend could be added for better understanding. Write down the names of all the village mappers.

Types of Mapping

Social Map or Social Profile : The social map is made by the farmers to describe locations of different castes and communities in the village, the conditions of households, roads and rivers etc. The social map forms a useful base for identifying problems of different households, their number and their characteristics. (Fig. 1)

Resource Map or Land Use pattern : The resource map of a village can show different kinds of natural resources. In a resource map, the villagers depict different kinds of rivers, ponds, trees, crop, animal species and the land utilization pattern. The problems can be discussed on the basis of a resource map. This can also form a basis for transect walk. (Fig. 2)

Fig. 1 : Social Map

Village : Purenatal

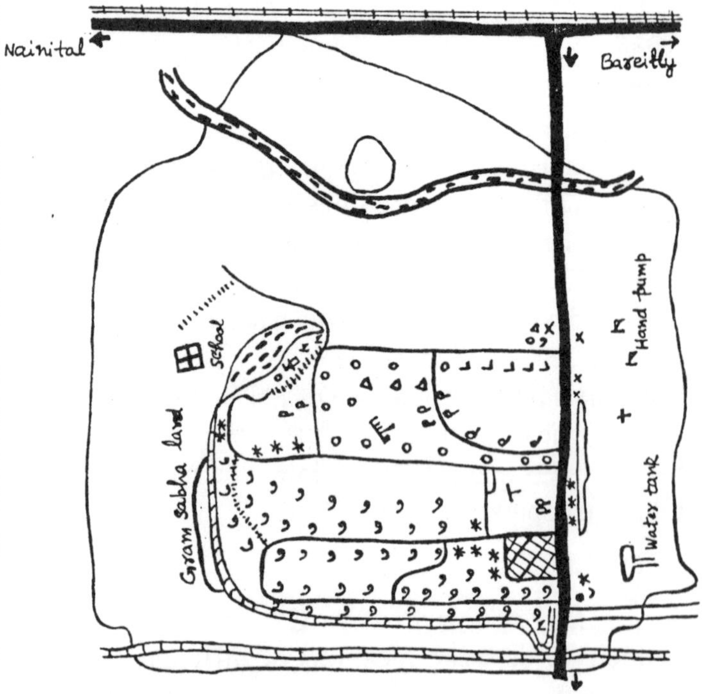

Legend :

Symbol	Caste	Symbol	Caste
6	Jatav	X	Teli
o	Jat	•	Balmiki
P	Pandit	+	Carpenter
Δ	Dheemar	T	Nat
*	Muslim	L	Kayasth

Informers : Farmers' Group

Fig. 2 : Land use Map

Village : Manda

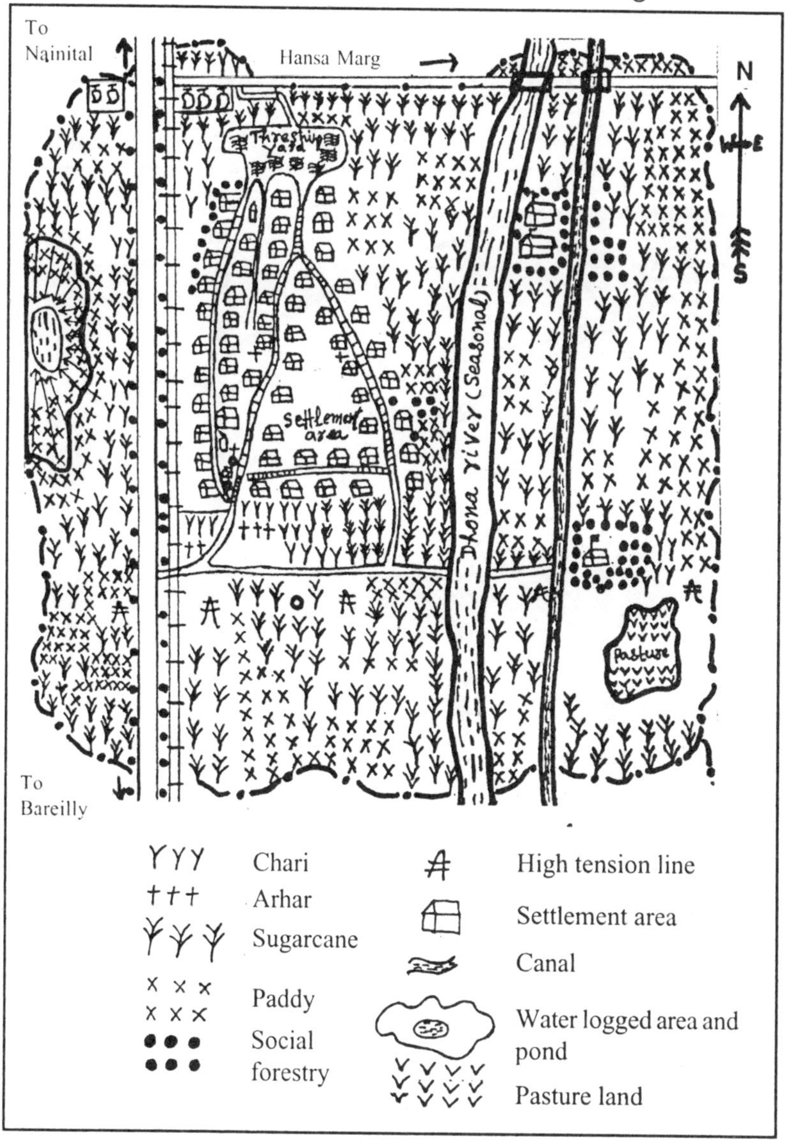

Informers : Farmers' Group

Occupational Map/Enterprise map : This map indicates the diversity of earnings. This type of map can be used for studying the income sources, expenditure pattern etc. (Figs. 3, 4)

Fig. 3 : Enterprise Map

Village : Purenatal

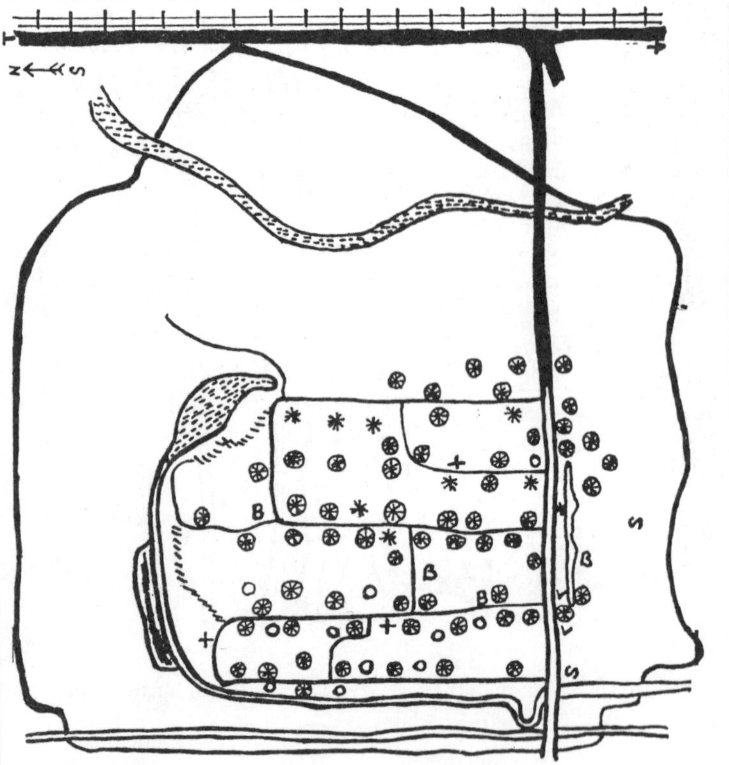

Legend :

- ✱ Farming + Dairy (Mainly cross bred)
- ⊛ Farming + Dairy (Mainly buffalo & local breeds
- + Farming + Dairy + Service
- $ Piggery + Labour
- o Farming + Labour
- B Labour + Goatery + other
- ✓ Labour (Landless)

Informers : Farmers

Fig. 4 : Enterprise Map

Village : Dohna

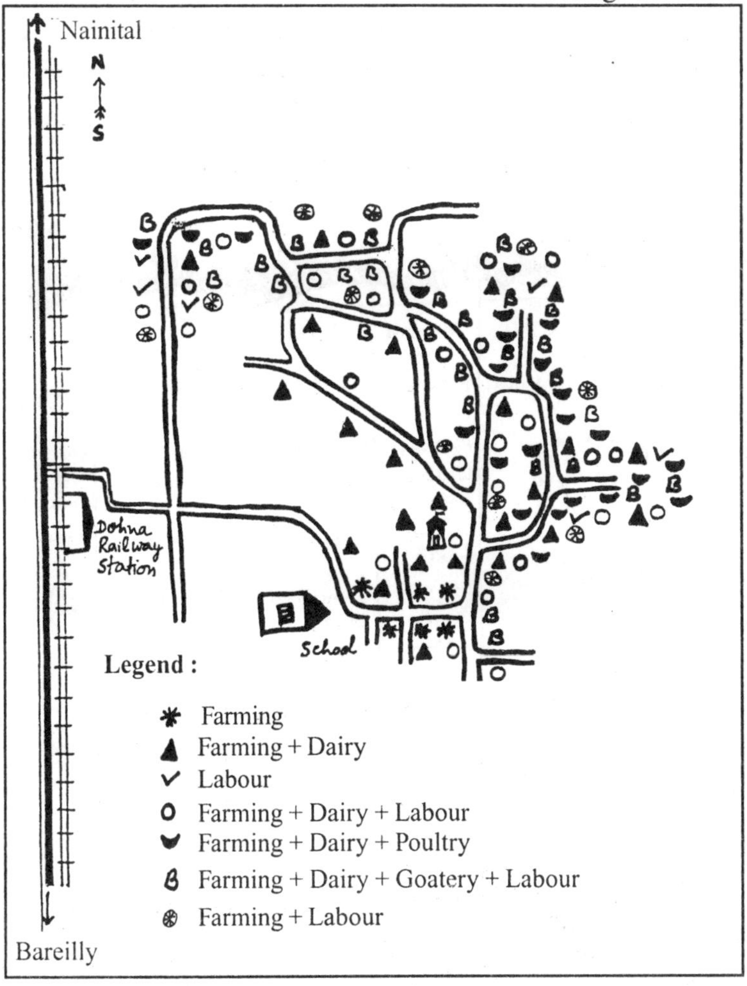

Informers : Farmers' Group

Transect Walk

A transect walk by PRA team across the village with villagers help to develop a clear idea on the natural resources, land use, vegetation, topography, cropping pattern, etc. It is a useful method to know rural ecological conditions. A walk from one point of the village to another enables the outsider to observe difficult aspects of rural ecology and to discuss with rural people about soil conditions, land use pattern, crop, livestock, agro-ecological zones, water flows and water sheds etc. (Fig. 5)

Fig. 5 : Transect of Village-Dohna

E ↔ W

Land	Slop	Low level	Settlement	High level	Low level
Soil fertility	Third grade	First-grade	First-grade	Second grade	Third grade
Crops	Paddy, Wheat, Lentil	Paddy, wheat, Sugarcane Lentil, Lehta	Sugarcane, Paddy, wheat, Lentil, Lehta	sugarcane Wheat, Chari Lentil	water logged area, Wheat
Soil type	Sandy, Loam Clay loam	Loam, Sandy loam	Loam and Sandy loam Clay, Hard	Sandy loam	clay
Irrigation	Irrigated by boring	Irrigated by boring	Irrigated by boring	Irrigated by boring	Irri gated
Fodder Production	Chari, Berseem	Berseem	Berseem	Chari	-
Wild animals	Antilop, deer, rabbit, Jaikal	Antilop	Antilop	Antilop, rabbit	Anti lop, deer
Trees	Sheesham	—	Neem, Pakad, Banyan	Sheesham, Mulbery, Sagon, Mango Gulava, Jamun	mango, Sheesham
Shrubs	Pawar, Khairti	—	—	Pawar, Guma, Khairti, Labhera	Large makery, Pir grass

Informers:

Shri Ch. Pratap Singh
Shri Kamal Khan
Shri Nazir Khan
Shri Pati Ram

Steps :

- * Select a group of villagers having good knowledge on physical resources of the village.
- * Discuss with these selected villagers on the physical map of the village and mark the routes that they would like to follow during transect walk.
- * Distribute responsibilities to the team members.
- * Observe and record the minute details of all important things that you come across.
- * Use six helpers when talking to villagers i.e. what, when, how, where, why and who.
- * All team members must complete the full transect walk.
- * Collect the indigenous as well as scientific practices followed by villagers.
- * Travel slowly and patiently.
- * Record the names of informants.
- * After the completion of walk, sit down at a suitable place and record the information on paper.
- * Draw an illustrative diagram of the transect using the collected information.

Transect walk can concentrate on specific area. Transect for agriculture would observe the land use pattern, crops, soil types, crop insects and pests, weeds, irrigation sources, cropping pattern, etc. The walk would have more emphasis on walk in the fields rather than in the village lanes. On the other hand transect walk for animal science would concentrate visits on animal species in the village houses and lanes. It may not be exactly straight from east to west or from north to south but will concentrate on animal herds. It may include fields also for pasture and fodder situations.

Time Analysis

Time analysis show the quantitative and qualitative changes overtime and can be used for many variables such as area and yields of different crops, livestock population, farming practices, variety, breeds, use of fertilizer and other inputs etc. In the method of time-line, elderly people are chosen as key informants. They narrate the history on different parameters. Triangulation may be done with the secondary data obtained from records.

Time line

Time line is a method of knowing history of major recollected events in a community. This method is also known as historical time-line of a community. Time-line illustrates diagramatically the past events which the member of a community remembers as being significant to their livelihood. The historical time-line is narrated by elderly villagers in details with respect to the major changes, that have taken place in their society and has impact on their economic, social and agro-ecological life. (Fig. 6)

Steps:

* Develop rapport with elderly villagers by explaining them the objectives of visit clearly.
* Select such focus group from the village which could give correct information.
* Ask the group about major significant events in various fields that have affected their life pattern in past.
* Ask the group about the impact of these events on their past and present life style.
* Arrange the narrated major events and its impact in logical sequences and in tabular form.
* Each of these events should be triangulated/cross-checked by two or three other villagers.

Fig. 6 : Historical Time Line

HISTORICAL TIME LINE

Village - Dohna

Year	Events
1500	Village settled
1915	Cholera epidemic in village
1935	First cycle was purchased in the village and first Pucca house constructed
1949	Primary school started
1950	Pucca mosque constructed
1954	Power substation established
1957	Consolidation of land holding was done for the first time
1972	Flood came in the village
1974	Brick road was constructed
1980	Village was electrified
1982	Second time consolidation of land holding was done
1985	First TV set was purchased in the village
1995	First Gobar Gas Plant was installed

Informers: 1. Shri Pratap Singh 2. Shri Kamal Khan 3. Shri Rajpal 4. Shri Ziledar Khan

Changes and Trends or Time Trends

This tool of PRA is used for depicting quantitative changes over a time in different aspects of rural life. By applying this method one can see the increasing or decreasing trend of hardship in life of rural people. (Fig. 7)

Steps :

* Obtain data from the focus group on a time frame about development in particular field
* Verify the provided data with other villagers.
* Arrange these information in tabular form and analyse clearly the increasing or decreasing trend
* Draw the conclusion of given data

Seasonal Analysis

Seasonal analysis helps in understanding seasonal cyclic variations in the selected parameters such as rainfall, temperature, humidity, cropping systems, crop rotations, labour availability, fodder availability, disease occurence etc. Seasonal analysis may be done through drawing of seasonal diagrames through PRA. The community members are asked to draw the diagram for a given year preferably starting from first month to say kharif season i.e. July and upto the month of June. If required each month may be divided into two fort nights or four weeks. Each activity or event is shown with the help of a bar drawn across the month. The diagram drawn by the community members on the ground is then transferred on the papers.

Steps:

* Brief the villagers or the focus group about the item with regard to which you require information. For instance, duration of crops, occurance of crop pests and diseases, occurance of livestock diseases and fodder availability in a calendar year.

Fig. 7 : Changes and Trends

Village : Dohna

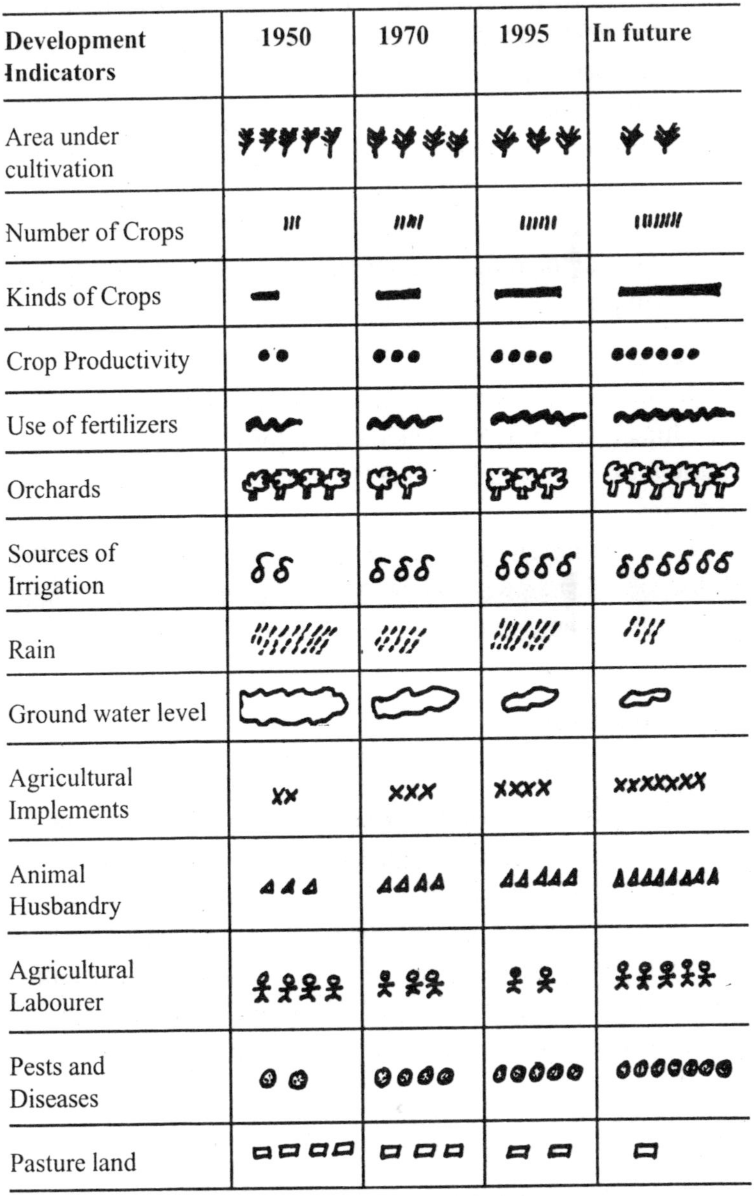

Informers : Farmers' Group

* Do all necessary preparations required for drawing a diagram.
* Tell them to enlist the crop or livestock disease that have affected their crops or livestock in previous years.
* Prapare a table and write down the name of the diseases on the first column on different rows.
* Write down the names of each month/season on the first row in different columns.
* Show this table to the focus group and ask them to depict the months in which a particular disease occur in a year.

Seasonal analysis helps in drawing out the information about the months/seasons in a year when the villagers face the hardships/problems. Such analysis helps the researchers and policy makers in formulating the projects to solve the rural problems.

The seasonal snalysis can be done for rainfall, seasonality of diseases, seasonwise work load in agriculture and animal husbandry, seasonwise work load of farmwomen, fuel availability, fooder availability etc. (Fig. 8, 9, 10, 11).

Matrix Ranking

Matrix ranking helps in comparing two or more objects in respect of perceived attributes or criteria by the villagers. In this exercise, different attributes and criteria are listed which are ranked either on the basis of fixed scoring or free sçoring according to their relative importance. It helps in understanding different criteria against which the villgers rank any particular object/ item, eg. crops, varietes or crops, livestock species, breeds of livestock, fodders and their varieties etc. (Fig. 12, 13, 14, 15).

Steps :

* Decide the topic (s) on which you would like villagers to score.

Fig. 8 : Seasonal Analysis of Animal Diseases

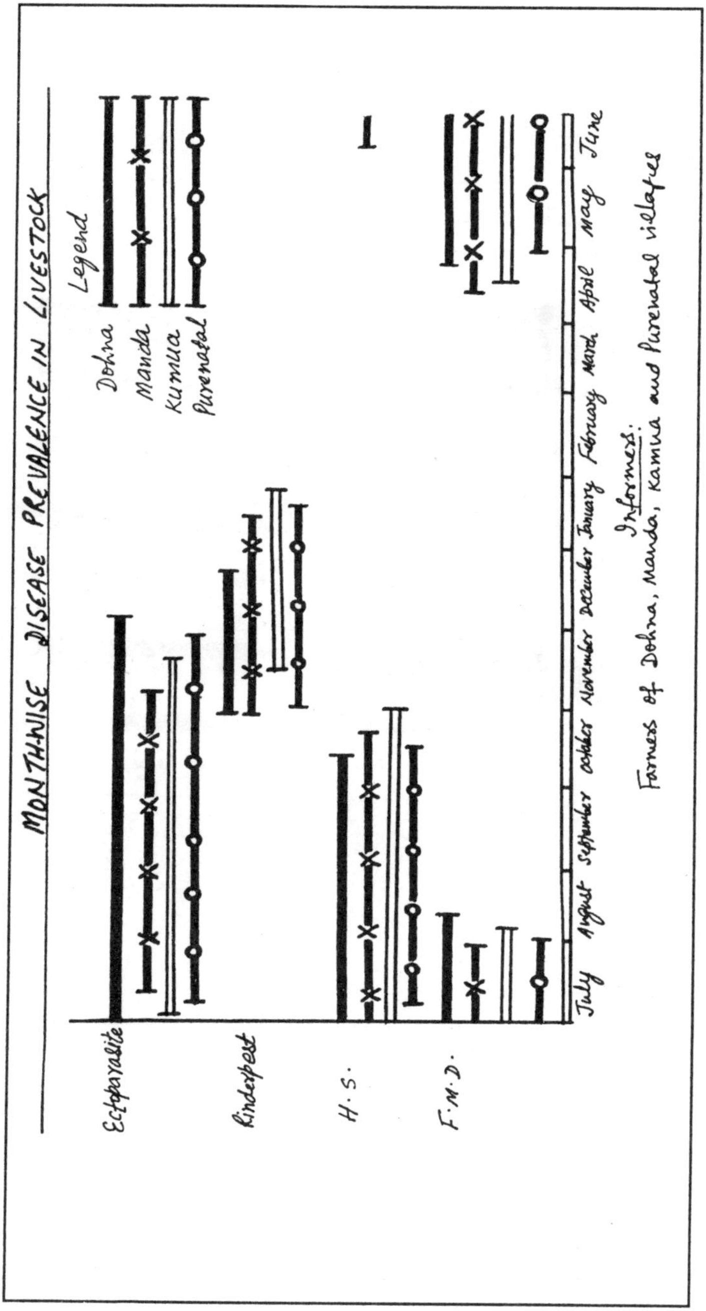

Fig. 9 : Seasonal Analysis of Pests & Diseases in Crops

Village : Purenatal

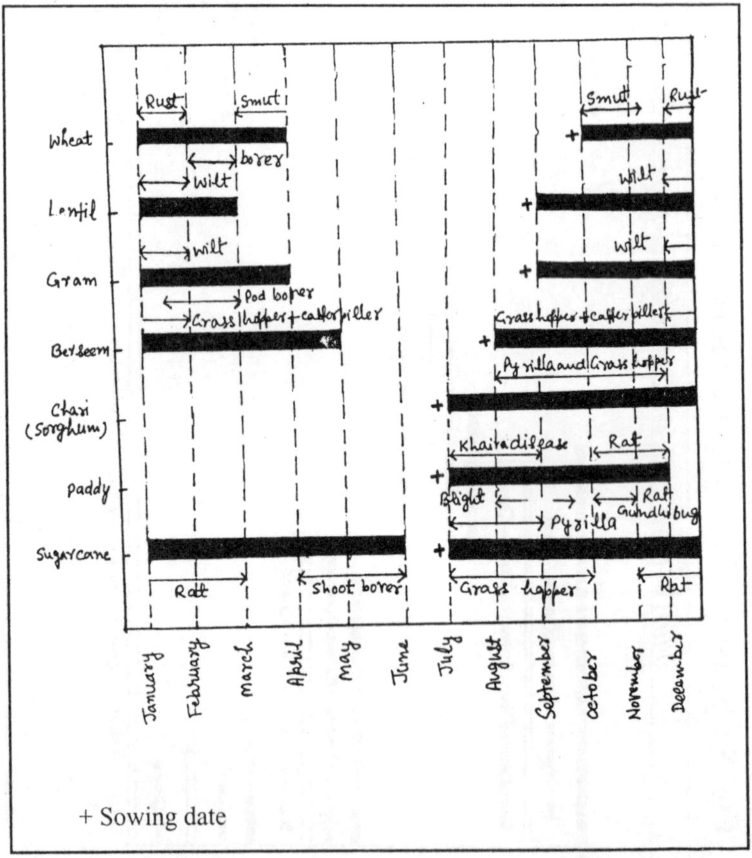

Informers : Sh. Babu Ram, Sh. Swaroop Singh, Sh. Narendra Singh

Fig. 10 : Seasonal Analysis of Work Load of Farm Women

Village : Dohna

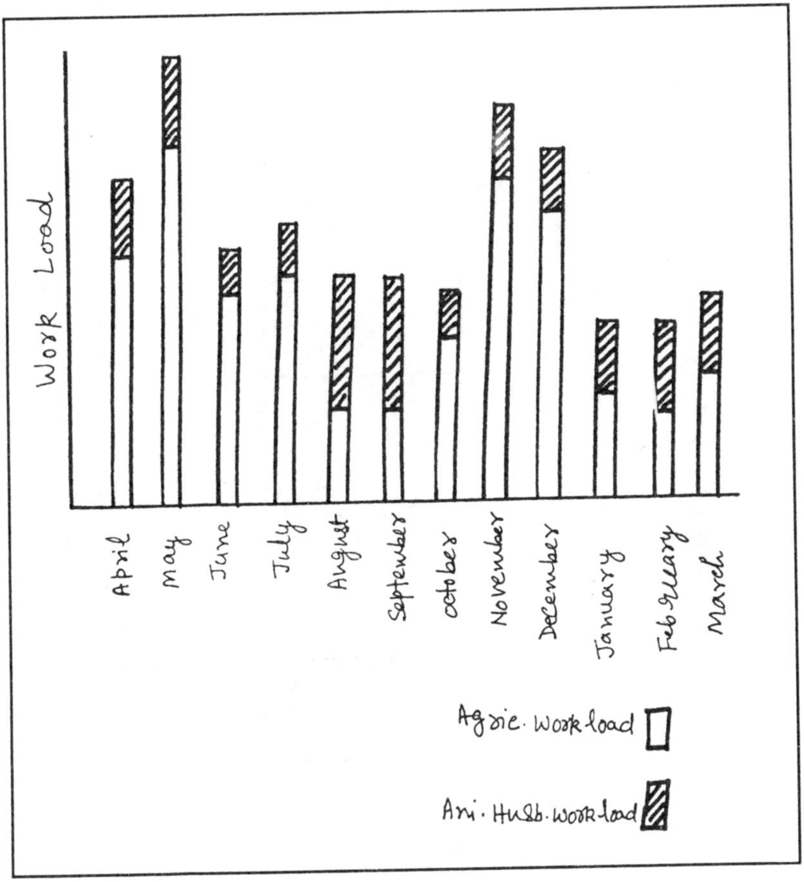

Informers : Smt. Hajra Begum, Smt. Vimla Yadav, Smt. Rajeshwari Yadav

Fig. 11: Green Fodder Availability

Village : Purenatal

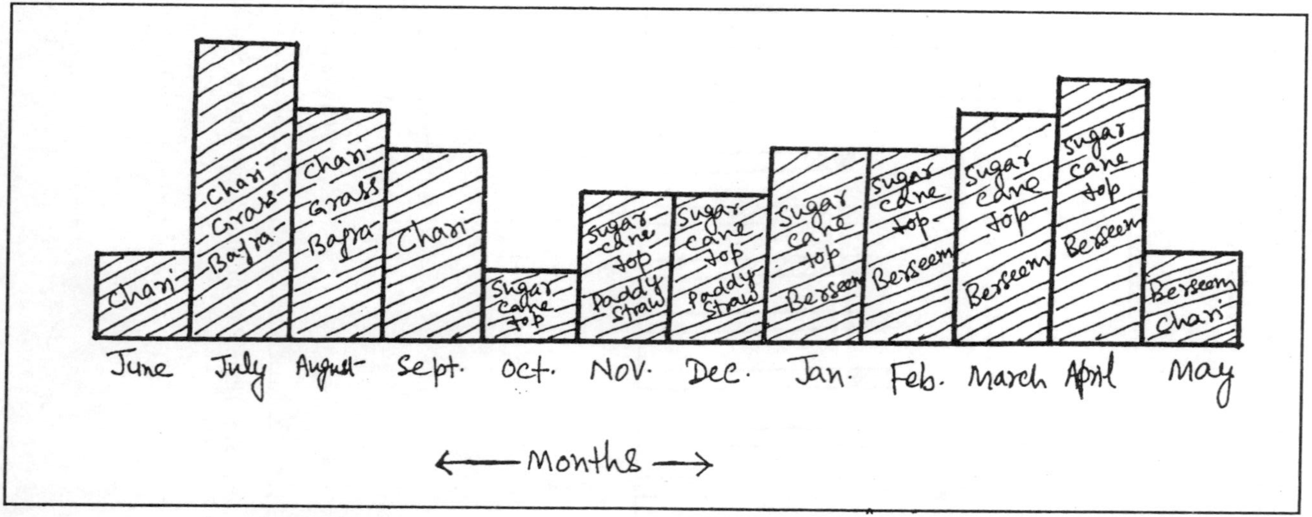

Informers : Shri Bhumi Prakash, Shri Hari Shankar Shri Naresh Chand

Fig. 12 : Matrix Ranking of Livestock and Poultry Production

Village : Manda

Village - Manda				
Kinds of Animals / Criteria	Cattle Production	Buffalo Production	Goat Production	Poultry Production
Use in farm operations	••••	•••	–	–
Milk yield	•••	••••	••	–
Meat Production	–	–	••••	•••
For manure	•••	••••	••	•
For eggs	–	–	–	••••
For drafting	•••	••••	–	–
Productive age duration	•••	••••	••	•
Additional income	•••	••••	•	••
Ranks	II	I	IV	III

Informers: Shri Durga Pal
Shri Ahmad Husain
Shri Balkar Singh

Fig. 13 : Matrix Ranking of Crops

Village : Manda

Crops / Criteria	Kharif			Rabi				
	Sugar cane	Paddy	Arhar	Wheat	Masoor	Lahi	Arhar	Sugar cane
More Straw / Fodder	•••	••	•	•••	••	••	•	•••••
Less Lodging	•	••	•••	••••	•••••	••	•••	•
Less Disease	••	•	••	•••	•••••	•••••	••	••
Less insect-attack	•••	•	••	••••	•••••	••	•	•••
More storage duration	•	•	•	••	•	•••••	•••	•
Taste	•••	•	••	••••	•••	••	••••	•••••
Short duration	•	•••	••	•••	••••	•••••	••	•
Drought resistance	••	•	•••	••	•••••	•••	••••	•••
Less water requirement	••	•	•••	••	•••••	•••	••••	•
More yield	•••	••	•	••••	•••	••	•	•••••
More income	•••	•	•	•	•••	••••	••	•••••
Net-profit	•••	•	••	•	•••••	•••	••	••••
Ranks	I	III	II	IV	I	II	V	III

Informers:

Farmers' Group

Fig. 14 : Matrix Ranking of Paddy Varieties

Village : Dohna

Variety Criteria	**Indrasan**	**Pant-4**	**Basmati**	**I.R. 24**
More yield	✱ ✱ ✱	✱ ✱ ✱ ✱	✱	✱ ✱
Less Diseases	● ●	● ●	● ● ● ●	● ● ●
Better taste	x x x	x	x x x x	x x
Less fertilizer requirement	ȣ ȣ	ȣ	ȣ ȣ ȣ ȣ	ȣ ȣ
Less insects	+ +	+ + + +	+ +	+ +
Ranks	II	III	I	IV

Rank: Basmati I
Indrasan II
Pant-4 III
I.R. 24 IV

- Have an initial discussion with the interested villagers and set the climate for discussion.
- Ask the villagers to list different alternative objects/ items such as breeds, varieties, species etc. Ask them to write on horizontal line to have columns.
- Ask them the possible criteria for ranking or preference and to write them on the left side column in vertical order to make rows.
- Draw the table of matrix by drawing horizontal lines dividing the possible criteria and vertical lines dividing the different objects / items.

Fig. 15 : Matrix Ranking of Sugarcane Varieties

Village : Dohna

Varieties / Criteria	Early varieties		Late maturing varieties			
	COS 8436	COS 64	COS 91269	COS 90269	COS 767	COS 7918
More income	o o	o	o o o	o o	o o o o	o
More tillering	o o	o	o o o	o o	o o	o o o o
More sugar	o o o o	o o o o	o o o	o o o	o o o	o o
Good for Ratoon crop	o o	o	o o o	o o o	o o o o	o
Less insects	o o o o	o	o o	o	o o	o
Better price	o o o o	o o o o	o o o	o o o	o o o o	o o o o
Less cost of production	o	o o	o o	o	o o o o	o o o

Ranks :

Early varieties :

COS 8436 - I

COS 64 - II

Late maturing varieties

COS 767 - I

COS 91269 - II

COS 7918 - III

COS 90269 - IV

Informers:

Shri ch. Pratap Singh

Shri. Kamal Khan

Shri. Yadvendra Singh

* Start talking about the first criteria and ask them to score out of 10 for each object / item. The most preferred object may have the highest score on the criteria.
* Move to the next criteria and ask them to score each object against that criteria. Complete for all the listed criteria.
* Triangulate the information with other villagers.
* Also ask the villagers for their best choice of the object/ item and record for its verification.
* Transfer the information on the sheet of paper.
* Calculate the total score for each object/item and triangulate with the best choice of object by the villagers.

Other PRA tools

Livelihood analysis

Livelihood analysis helps in obtaining information about decisions and problems and also the coping strategies of different households in relation to socio-economic factors.

This type of analysis can be used for studying the household size, composition, income and expenditure pattern, income from different sources etc.

Steps :

* Decide on the topic with respect to which livelihood analysis is to be carried out such as income and expenditure pattern for different types of household.
* Decide on the classification of household in terms of socio-economic categories, caste categories etc.
* Choose a representative household from different socio-economic categories.
* Ask the head of the chosen household for different

sources of income and ask him to show it in the form of a pie diagram by showing the income from different sources (Fig. 16).

Fig. 16 : Livelihood Analysis

Village : Manda

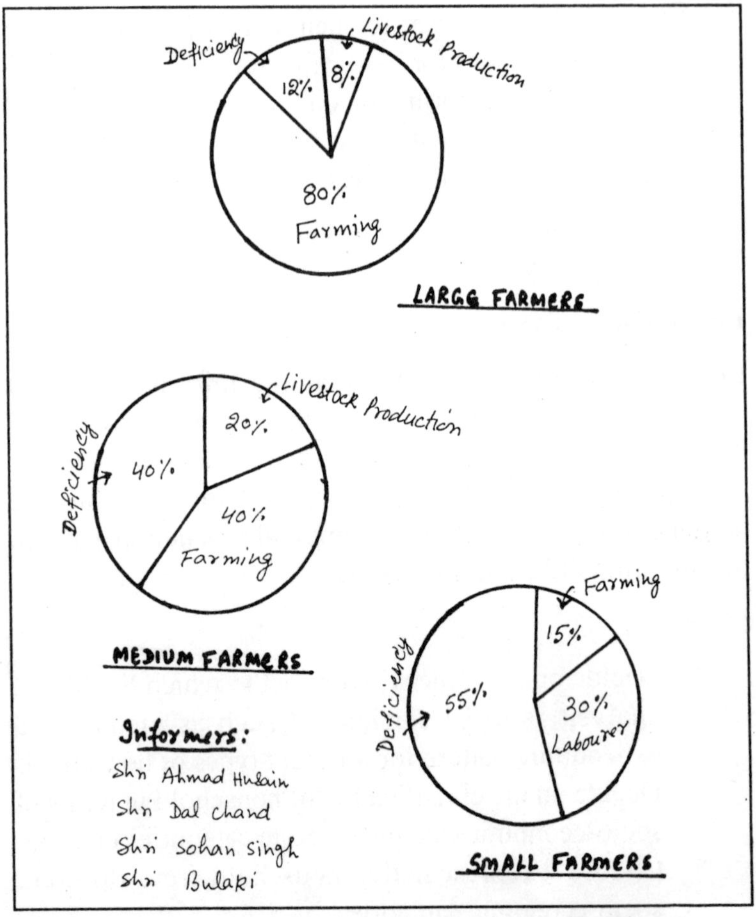

Village Institution Linkage Map (Venn or Chapati Diagram)

Venn diagram is a visual method to represent the role and relationship of individuals and institutions, their degree of importance and relationship with other individuals and institutions. The individual or institution are depicted by circles and their importance by the size of circles. The relationship is depicted by connecting lines and distance of placement. Different aspects of decision making relationship can be studied by venn diagram. The villagers are asked to enumerate various institutions contributing to a specific action, project or desision - making. They are asked to place them in the form of circle, the size on the basis of importance and the distance indicating the relationship among each other. (Fig. 17)

Indigenous Technical Knowledge

Rural people have an intimate knowledge of many aspects of their surroundings. Over centuries, people have learnt how to grow crops, how to maintain animals, what varieties to plant, when to sow seeds, which plant is poisonous and which can be used as medicine, how to cure disease and so on. These indigenous technical knowledge (ITK) have been generated by local people through a series of innumerable informal experiments. ITK is local knowledge that is dynamic but unique to a given culture or society. Local people are the custodians of this indigenous knowledge systems. ITKs are based on human experiences and are tested in most cases over centuries of use. These are holistic and integrated with culture. ITKs are useful as these are the basis for self-sufficiency and self determination. It draws on local resources. It provides effective alternatives to scientific know how. It reduces cost burden as these are often use local resources and are cheaper.

Fig. 17 : Venn (Chapati) Diagram

Village : Manda

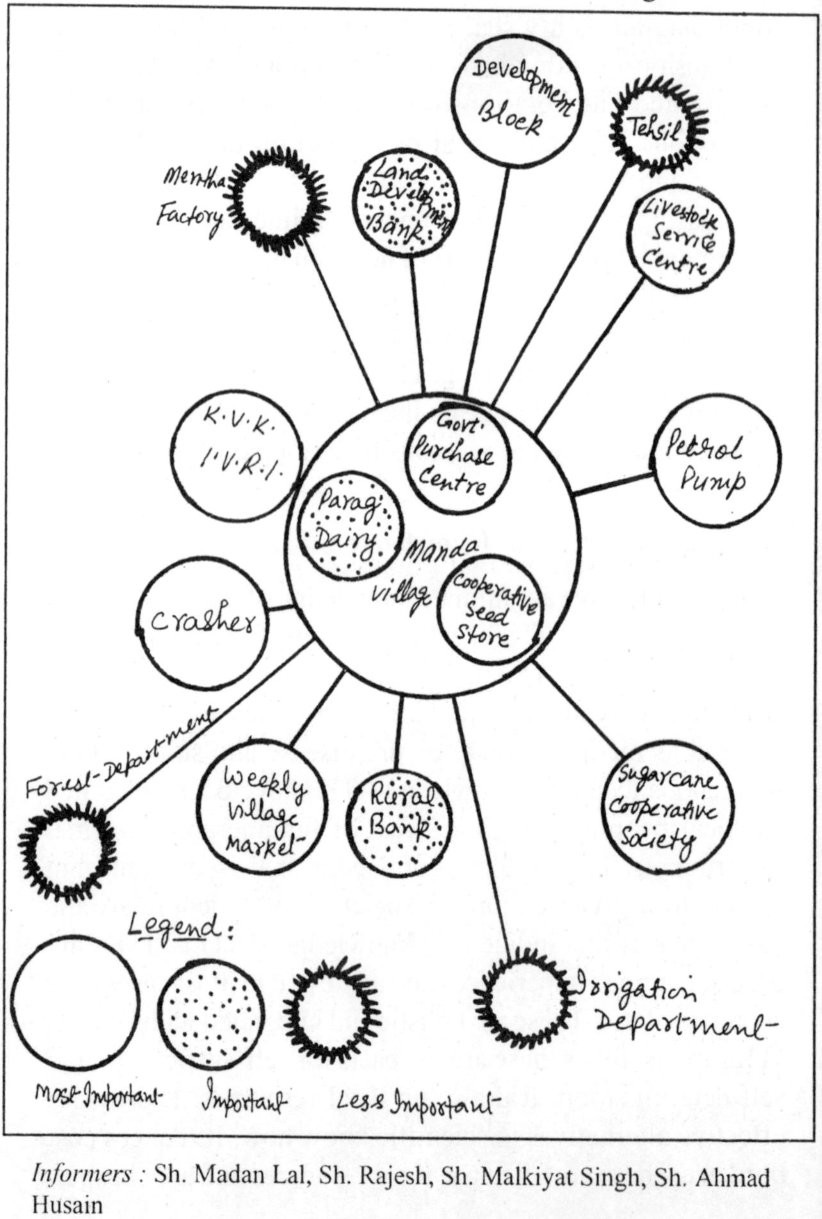

Informers : Sh. Madan Lal, Sh. Rajesh, Sh. Malkiyat Singh, Sh. Ahmad Husain

Indigenous Technical knowledge (ITKs) can best be collected and documented through PRA tools. Since, the ITKs are generated, developed and tested by the local people through a series of experimentation, these can well be validated for their efficiency through the knowledge of the key informants or local exeperts. Some of the Indigenous technical knowledge (ITKs) in the field of animal science are listed below:

Indigenous Technical Knowledge in Animal Husbandry

H.S. Control:

- The paste of kala Jeera is applied on and around the swelling part of the H.S. affected animals.
- Hot water treatment also helps to reduce the swelling area of animal affected with H.S.

F.M.D. Control:

- The paste of Jamun and Babool bark is applid onthe hooves of FMD affected animals
- Oral extract of 2.50 leaves of Akoa and 2.50 leaves of bitter guard is given to animals in FMD.
- Use of tobacco powder, Gur & red chillies and fresh fish meal in animal diet help the control of FMD in animals.
- Use of alum water for mouth wash and Alum water & Ghee for affected wound in foot helps the animals to recover.
- Babool barks' extract also acts like antiseptic agent when the FMD affected parts are washed with it.
- The extract of peach leaves is mixed with milk and is applied 3 times daily on the wounds to heal the animals from FMD.
- An applicaton of Anjeer leaves in skimmed milk three times a day helps to heal the wounds.

- Phenyl washing is also followed in affected foot of the animals.

R.P. Control :

To control Rinderprest in animal, farmers use the mixture of barley flour and grind shisham leaves are mixed and fed to the affected animal orally.

Diarrhoea Treatment :

- The juice of stone fruit (Bel) mixed with water is drenched to check the diarrhoea - starch of rice and barley flour bolus is given to the diarrhoea affected animals orally to check the dehydration.
- Dry Bhusa and the wheat flour mixed with water is drenched/ fed two times a day to recover the affected animal from the diarrhoea.

Bloat :

- To control the bloat, mixture of ground onion and mustard oil is given orally to the bloat affected animals

Parasitic Control :

- Rice starch is pasted on the ticks affected skin of the cattle and buffalo.
- Dry red chillies are applied on the tick affected area of the skin of cattle and buffalo.
- Neem leaves + mustard oil are used to treat the animal against the internal worm infestation.
- Papaya seeds are also used to treat the internal worm infestation of animals.

Fever Control :

- The extract of Gumma (weed) mixed with skimmed milk is fed to reduce the temperature.

Mastitis Treatment :

- The fermentatin of boiled, green chenopodium album (Bathua) in 1 litre of water, controls the mastitis in cattle and buffalo.

Anoestrous Management:

- To induce oestrus, pigeon waste is given orally to heifers for showing heat symptoms clearly.

Quantifying Indigenous Knowledge (QuIk) - A Method Based on Matrix Ranking

QuIk develops the PRA tool matrix ranking to access farmers technical knowledge in order to test hypothesis about agricultural performance.

Criteria for the matrix are defined in order to test a hypothesis, which may itself be derived from interactive farmer - researcher discussion. The matrix after development is used as the basis for the interviews with a series of independent key informants. These key informants or experienced farmers are identified through informal inquiry in the village.

After introduction between researchers and key informants/ interviewees, the interview process is initiated by drawing matrix table on the ground and labelling the columns and rows with appropriate locally available material. The treatments / criteria are carefully explained to the interviewee to ensure that all the respondents refer to the same parameters. The criteria are defined in terms of farmers' own experience.

The farmer is then asked to score crop performance (using stones or other available counters) against the different criteria. This process is initiated by asking where the crop performs the best and where the crop performs the worst. A set number of stones is provided and the interviewee is asked to allocate these first to the best and worst cases and then allocate to the remaining cases accordingly. The number may range from 0 to worst to 10 to the best. Periodic probing is required to ensure that the informant understands the criteria as intended.

After the matrix has been completed the farmer is asked to explain the reasoning behind his decision about the different scores. The farmer should be allowed to modify his initial scoring. The same matrix table is used to interview other key informants. Each farmer must be interviewed in isolation from other key informants in order that each matrix table can be considered as a discrete event. Further, it is better that the interview is conducted by a team of scientists to strengthen triangulation and peer checks.

After completing the interview with 10 to 20 key informants, the data are compiled and subejcted to statistical analysis as in case of experimental design. The data could be subjected to ANOVA test or 't' test for testing the significance of difference.

Example : Qulk matrix for assessing the performance of two ginger varieties in different levels of shades and fertility.

Criteria	Local ginger	Mainland ginger
Shaded / High fertility	000	000
Shaded /Medium fertility	0000000	0000000000
Shaded / Low fertility	0000	00000000
Sunlight/High fertility	00	0000
Sunlight/Medium fertility	000	00000
Sunlight/Low fertility	00	000

3

Participatory Planning

After sharing and analysis of all the information collected from the villagers using different PRA tools, the process of participatory planning may be initiated. In this exercise, efforts are made to involve the villagers in developing a plan for action using their resources in best possible manner. The villagers come-up with their own views in planning their own future activities and offer suggestions.

The villagers are asked to identify and prioritize their problems and suggest possible solutions / interventions.

Steps:

* Arrange display all the information collected through PRA exercises in presentable form (maps, chart etc.)
* Arrange meeting with villagers at a convenient time and place.
* Allow the villagers to look and discuss their own analysis and drawing prepared by themselves during PRA exercises.
* If possible arrage a presentation of results by villagers to a large group.
* After sufficient discussion on existing situations, ask the villagers to identify the problems of their village. Ask one villager to write each problem on separate piece of paper.
* The villagers arrange the problems (by putting the pieces of papers on the ground) according to their priority / severity.

* Allow sometime to prioritize the problems by villagers.
* Initiate the discussion on the first problem and ask the villagers to indicate the possible causes.
* Keep the problem in the centre and its causes around it and connect with the help of arrows.
* The socio-economic causes may be placed towards left, while bio-physical causes may be placed towards right of the problem.
* Ask the villagers about the reasons of the causes indicated. These could be considered as secondary causes.
* Ask the tertiary causes also in the same manner and complete the problem - cause diagram for each problem one by one.
* Ask the villagers to identify the causes, which could be removed / tackled/ managed by the villagers within the available resources.
* Prioritize the causes in respect of managing them easily.
* Ask the villagers to suggest solutions or the ways to manage the cause. Alternate solutions may be noted.
* Have discussions on the alternative solutions and let the villagers decide for action.
* Enlist each action plan and consolidate the entire plan along with the responsibilities fixed for each action.
* Have second meeting of villagers and arrange presentation of action plan by the villagers before the large group (Fig. 18, 19, 20, 21, 22).

Fig. 18 : Participatory Planning

Village : Kamua

Problems	Cause	Efforts made to solve the problem	What the farmers want for solving the problem	No. of farmers to be benefited
(1)	(2)	(3)	(4)	(5)
1. Unemployment/ Underemployment (youth and women)	- Lack of knowledge on agro based enterprise - No other work	No effort	knowledge and skill of- - Dairying - Poultry - Fishery - Candle making - Agarbatti making	 30 5 2 15 15
2. Low sale price of agricultural produce	Crops not grown for seed production	No effort	Seed Production Technology	35
3. Low yield of sugarcane	- Lodging - Stem borer	- No effort - Insecticide was not effective	- Availability of lodging resistant variety of sugarcane - Method of sugarcane tyeing - Effective insecticide	All farmers

Contd...

Fig. 18 : (*Contd.*)

(1)	(2)	(3)	(4)	(5)
4. Low yield of paddy	- Lack of timely availability of irrigation - Prevalence of disease - Gundhi insect attack	- Irrigation in the absence of rain - No effort - Burning of type in paddy fields	- Availability of canal water - Disease resistant varietes - Knowledge of Gundhi insect control.	All farmers
5. Low yield of wheat	- Lack of improved variety seed - Prevalence of Phalaris minor - Smut disease - Lack of know-ledge of balanced fertilizer	- Seed purchased from Govt. seed store but poor germination - Weedcide used but less effective - No effort	- Improved good seed -Method of weed control - knowledge of plant protection - Knowledge of balanced fertilizer	All farmers
6. Low yield of lentil	Wilt disease	- No effort	- Knowledge of disease resistant variety and control of disease	All farmers
7. Low yield of mustard	- Aphid attack - Only urea is used - Thining not done	- No effort	- Knowledge on aphid control - Knowledge on balanced fertilizer - Knowledge about thining	All farmers

Contd...

Fig. 18 : (*Contd.*)

(1)	(2)	(3)	(4)	(5)
8. Low fruiting of mangoes	- Insect attack like Bhunga, Gundhi and aphid - Disease in flowers - Dense orchard - Lack of manuring	No effort	- Knowlodge of insect management - knowledge of disease control - Knowledge of method of manuring in orchand - Knowledge of proper plantation of mango	All mango farmers
9. Low milk yield	- Local breeds - Lack of green fodder	No effort	- High yielding breeds of cattle and buffalo - Knowledge of high production of green fodder	30 farmers
10. Other problem and causes of low production in agriculture	- Lack of bullocks - Broadcasting method of sowing - Lack of avalability of diesel and urea in the required season	No effort	- Tractor drawn ferti seed drill - Availability of diesel and urea at proper time in the required season	14 farmers

Informer : Farmers' group

Fig. 19 : Prioritisation of Major Problems

Village : Purenatal No. of Families : 182

Sl. No.	Problem	Area wise distribution of problem	Importance of Enterprise	Seriousness of problem	No. of affected families	Relative importance of the problem
1.	Low yield of Sugarcane	XXXX	XXX	XXXX	125	II
2.	Low yield of Paddy	XXX	XXX	XXX	125	IV
3.	Low Yield of Wheat	XXX	XXX	XXX	116	V
4.	High disease and pest prevalence in Mango	X	XX	XXX	12	XII
5.	Low yield of pulses	XX	XX	XXXX	48	VIII
6.	Low milk yield in cattle and buffalo	XXX	XXX	XXX	80	VI
7.	High mortality of cattle and buffalo calf	XX	XX	XXX	101	I
8.	Low conception rate of A.I.	XXXX	XXX	XXX	117	VII
9.	High disease prevalence in live-stock	XXXX	XXXX	XXXX	126	III
10.	Poor economic condition of Women	XX	X	XX	64	XI
11.	fodder scarcity	XXX	XX	XX	80	IX
12.	Infertility in cows	XX	XXX	XXX	45	X

Legends: XXXX-Very important, XXX-Important, XX-Less important, X-least important Village facilitator: Group of farmers

Fig. 20 : No. of Households affected and the Ranking of Problems in the Selected Villages

No. of Families : 665

Sl. No.	Problems	Problem Ranking				No. of Affected Families				Total
		Dohna	Manda	Kamua	Purenatal	Dohna	Manda	Kamua	Purenatal	
1.	Low yield of sugarcane	II	I	I	II	194	88	73	125	480
2.	Low yield of paddy	I	II	II	IV	213	82	64	125	484
3.	Low yield of wheat	IV	VII	VI	V	189	78	62	116	445
4.	High pest and disease in mango	XI	—	III	XII	12	—	25	12	49
5.	Low yield of pulses	IX	V	X	VIII	60	53	21	48	182
6.	Low milk yield in cattle and buffalo	V	IV	V	VI	181	79	61	80	401
7.	High disease prevalence in live-stock	III	III	IV	I	169	83	57	126	435
8.	High mortality of cattle and buffalo calf	VI	VIII	VII	VII	140	73	48	101	362
9.	Low conception rate of A.I.	VIII	X	XI	III	85	49	46	117	297
10.	Poor economic condition of women	X	IX	IX	XI	145	52	45	64	306
11.	Lack of green fodder availability	XII	VI	VIII	IX	181	79	61	80	401
12.	Infertility in cows	—	—	—	X	25	21	18	45	109

Fig. 21 : Problem-Cause Diagram

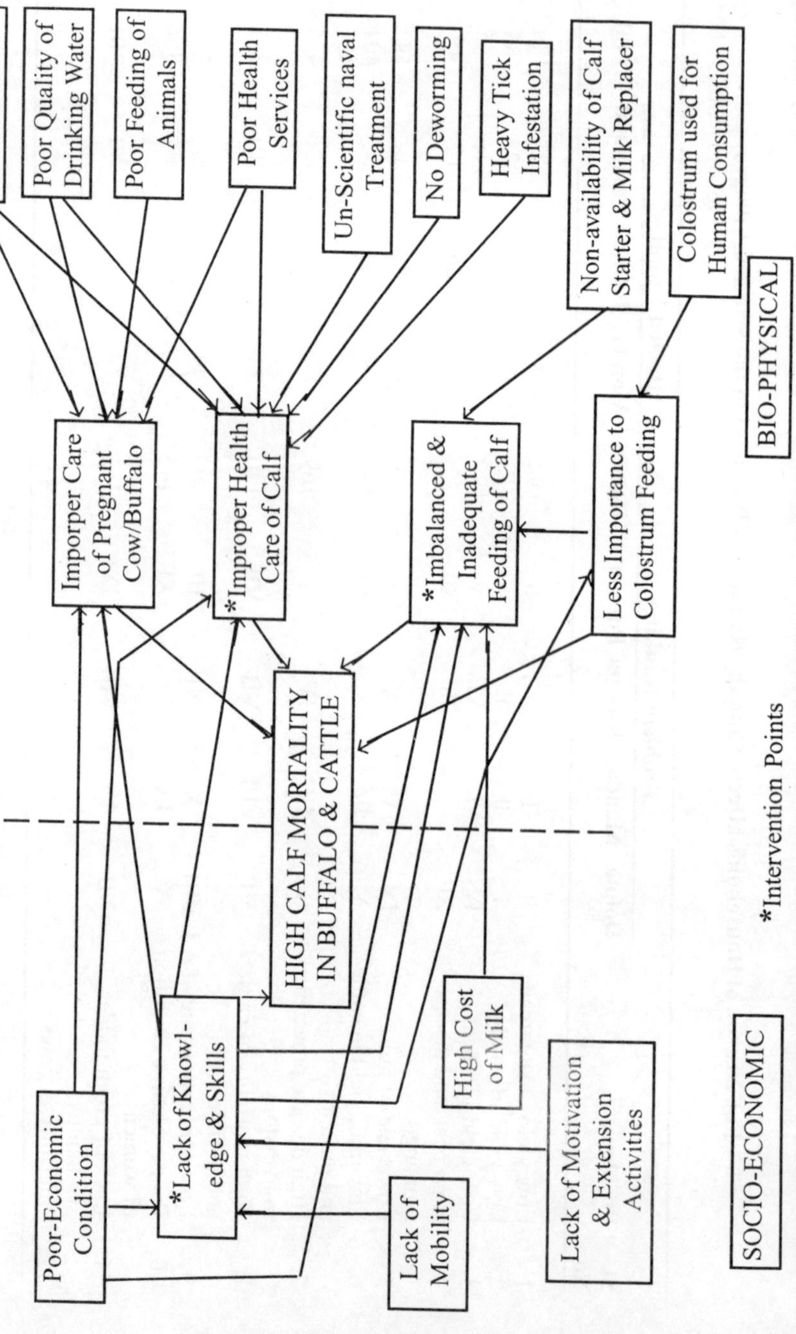

Fig. 22 : Problem-Cause Diagram

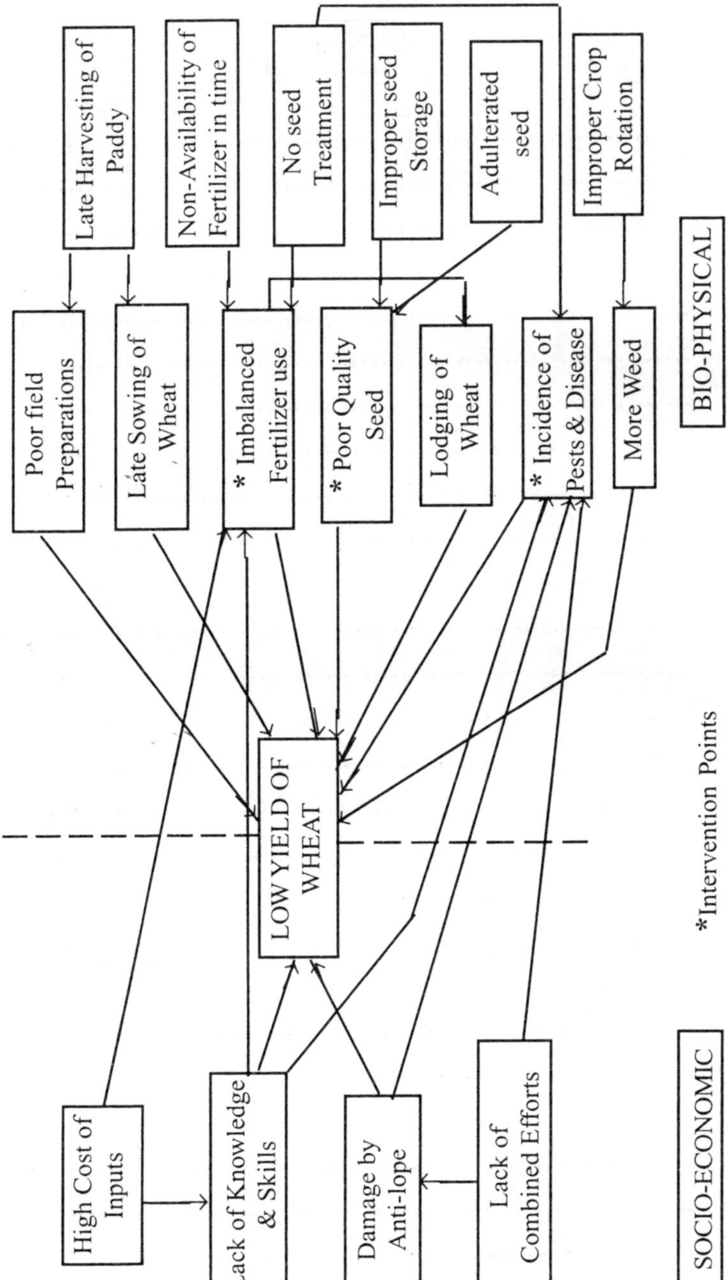

Notes

Notes

Notes